Thirty-Day Devotions
for the Holy Souls

Thirty-Day Devotions for the Holy Souls

Susan Tassone

Our Sunday Visitor Publishing Division
Our Sunday Visitor, Inc.
Huntington, Indiana 46750

Nihil Obstat
Reverend William Woestman, O.M.I., J.C.D.
Censor Deputatus
December 5, 2003

Imprimatur
Most Reverend Edwin M. Conway, D.D.
Vicar General
Archdiocese of Chicago
December 10, 2003

The *Nihil Obstat* and *Imprimatur* are official declarations that a book is free of doctrinal and moral error. No implication is contained therein that those who have granted the *Nihil Obstat* and *Imprimatur* agree with the content, opinions, or statements expressed. Nor do they assume any legal responsibility associated with publication.

Every reasonable effort has been made to determine copyright holders of excerpted materials and to secure permissions as needed. If any copyrighted materials have been inadvertently used in this work without proper credit being given in one form or another, please notify Our Sunday Visitor in writing so that future printings of this work may be corrected accordingly.

Our Sunday Visitor Publishing Division
Our Sunday Visitor, Inc.
200 Noll Plaza
Huntington, IN 46750

ISBN: 978-1-59276-052-7 (Inventory No. T103)
LCCN: 2003113165

Cover design by Monica Haneline
Cover art by M. Müller
Interior design and art by Garrett Fosco

PRINTED IN THE UNITED STATES OF AMERICA

To Jesus,
Thank you from my heart.

Table of Contents

Acknowledgments

THE MOST OUTSTANDING collections on purgatory in the United States are provided by the University of Saint Mary of the Lake, Mundelein, Illinois, and Loyola University Chicago. I am most grateful to the staffs for their assistance.

I am most deeply grateful to the "purgatory authors" who made this work possible. Their eloquent prose is timeless. Their writings inspire, encourage, and show their love for the holy souls in purgatory. Their ardent desire for us to carry on this extraordinary devotion until the end of time is truly awe-inspiring:

• *Afterlife*, by Michael H. Brown, copyright © 1997, Faith Publishing (Santa Barbara, Calif.).
• *All About the Angels*, by Father Paul O'Sullivan, O.P. (E.D.M.), copyright © 1991, TAN Publishers (Rockford, Ill.).
• *Charity for the Suffering Souls*, by Rev. John A.

Nageleisen, copyright © 1994, TAN Publishers (Rockford, Ill.).

• *The Divine Crucible of Purgatory*, by Mother Mary of St. Austin, Helper of the Holy Souls (revised and edited by Nicholas Ryan, S.J.), copyright © 1940, P.J. Kenedy & Sons (New York).

• *Encounters With Silence*, by Karl Rahner, S.J. (tr. J.M. Demske, S.J.), copyright © 1969, Sands and Co. (London and Glasgow).

• *Fasting*, by Father Slavko Barbarić, O.F.M., copyright © 1988, Franciscan University Press (Steubenville, Ohio).

• *The Guardian Angels, Our Heavenly Companions*, copyright © 2001, TAN Publishers (Rockford, Ill.).

• *In Conversation with God, Daily Meditations, Volume Two: Lent and Eastertide*, by Francis Fernandez, copyright © 2000, Scepter Ltd. (London).

• *Lest We Forget*, by Very Rev. James Alberione, S.S.P., S.T.D., copyright © 1967, Daughters of St. Paul (Boston, Mass.).

• *Magnificat* (November, 2001; Vol. 3, No. 9), published by Pierre-Marie Dumont (Rockville, Md.).

• *The Month of the Holy Souls*, copyright © 1929,

• *Thoughts for all Times*, Rt. Rev. Msgr. John S. Vaughan, copyright ©1998, Little Flower Press (Front Royal, Va.).

I also want to express my deepest thanks to my publisher and the staff at Our Sunday Visitor. As always, they have been supportive and understanding, and they have resurrected the plight of the suffering souls in the hearts of the faithful.

Finally, I extend very special thanks to my support team in Chicago, especially Maureen Gregory, Pat Hackett, Larry Lesof, and Barb Matousek. They accompany me on speaking tours, listen to my ideas, and most importantly, pray for our holy heroes. We say together, echoing the prayer from the Easter Vigil:

Christ yesterday and today,
The beginning and the end,
Alpha and Omega.
All time belongs to Him,
And all the ages.
To Him be glory and power
Through every age forever.
Amen.

Foreword

MANY PEOPLE influence and shape the personal life of each one of us — father, mother, family members, friends, teachers, and countless others, some of whom we do not now remember. This is even more true for our life in Christ; as members of His Church, we are in a vital communion with the angels, with the saints, as well as with all those, living and dead, who are part of the People of God.

In this book, Susan Tassone reminds us of those linked to us by faith and grace who now, after their death, await the vision of God in the purifying situation of purgatory. They have died in God's grace and friendship, and are indeed assured of eternal salvation, but at death were not yet fully aligned with God's will for their perfection.

Purgatory is a topic that cannot be evaded if we are serious about the belief in the afterlife, which is integral to Christian teaching and which confronts us with a future that depends on our relationship with God in the moment of death. What becomes of those people who accept the truth about God and about themselves as it is revealed in Christ and who have striven to live it but have died before they have been thoroughly transformed into the likeness of Christ? They belong to God but are not yet ready for a heaven of perfect love and communion with God. God forgives us our sins, but we have still to be made holy, fit for the fullness of life with God.

Some theologians have suggested that the necessary purification takes place in the act and experience of dying. This is not the traditional doctrine of the Church; it is not what the *Catechism of the Catholic Church* tells us when it says that those who need it "after death ... undergo purification" (*CCC*, no. 1030); nor is it in accord with that divine process of salvation which entails the progress and growth of our humanity in moral perfection, involving our cooperation as our will is brought into harmony with the will of God. It takes time for grace to penetrate the deep recesses of our complex character, weakened as it is by sin.

Purgatory is not explicitly present in Scripture; it is, however, a reasonable inference from important truths that are found there. It is a doctrine of the Catholic Church, even if not one of her central teachings, and is part of the deposit of faith, which calls for our assent and which should shape our lives as followers of Christ. From the earliest times, as archeological evidence in the Christian catacombs shows, belief in purgatory has been kept alive in the liturgy of the Church and in her pastoral practice; in every Mass, we remember those who have gone before us "marked with the sign of faith"; in Catholic funeral rites, we offer the eucharistic sacrifice, asking pardon for the sins and transgressions of the one who has died.

Though the situation of the departed is already determined by God's judgment at the moment of death, we can still assist them by offering prayers and good works on their behalf, begging that they, who are forever joined to us in the Communion of Saints, will benefit soon and more fully from Christ's victory over sin, that they may "achieve the holiness necessary to enter the joy of heaven" (*CCC*, no. 1030). Susan

Tassone's book will help us to pray for these holy souls and, as well, to seek their prayers on our behalf.

The Church is clear that purgatory exists as a gracious gift of God's love, but she says little about where or how this purification takes place or about its duration. In some measure, that is developed in the spiritual tradition of the Church, something of which is set out in this book; at the same time, Susan Tassone respects the limits of what we can know and avoids the exaggerations that, in the past, have been a source of division among Christians.

May the pages of this book inspire us to pray for the dead and to pray also for our own happy death.

+ Francis Cardinal George, O.M.I.
Archbishop of Chicago

Introduction

ST. FRANCIS DE SALES says, "We do not often enough remember our dead, our faithful departed." Thus, Holy Mother Church, like a good mother, consecrates the whole month of November to the memory of the dead. This pious practice of praying through an entire month for the dead takes rise from the earliest ages of the Church and was preached with zeal by all the great Church Fathers and Doctors.

Praying for the dead is clearly shown in Scripture. (For more details, see my book *The Rosary for the Holy Souls in Purgatory*.) The custom of mourning thirty days existed among the Jews. People mourned for Moses for thirty days. The celebration of the Mass for the Dead on the first, seventh, and thirtieth day was known as "Month's Mind." Pope St. Gregory the Great established the practice of saying thirty Masses on thirty consecutive days, and they are called Gregorian Masses.

I present these thirty days of devotions and invite you to become "burning bushes" of prayer for our beloved dead. St. Ambrose reminds us, "We have loved them dearly during life, so let us not abandon them until we have conducted them by our prayers into the house of the Lord."

How consoling that our golden links of prayer still unite us to those who "fall asleep in the Lord," and that we still can speak to them and pray for them!

"So then, brethren, stand firm and hold to the traditions which you were taught by us, either by word of mouth or by letter" (2 Thessalonians 2:15).

Embrace this devotion and spread it widely. God is never outdone in generosity!

Testament of St. Ephraem

LAY ME NOT with sweet spices,
    For this honor avails me not.
Nor yet use incense and perfumes,
    For the honor benefits me not;
Burn ye the incense in the holy place;
    As for me, escort me only with your prayers.
Give ye your incense to God,
    And over me send up hymns.
    Be mindful of me in your intercessions.
What can goodly odor profit
    To the dead who cannot perceive it?
Bring incense to burn in the holy place,
    That they who enter may smell the savor.
Wrap thou not the fetid carrion
    In silk that profits it nothing;
Cast it out upon the dunghill,
    For it finds no comfort in tributes of respect.

Come, my brothers, and lay out my remains;
    the decree has gone forth that I can tarry
    no longer.

Give me, as provision for my journey,
  Your prayers, your psalms, and your sacrifices.
When the number of thirty days is complete,
  Then, O my brothers, make remembrance
  of me.
For the dead truly derive succor,
  From the sacrifices offered up by the living.

Say you that the dead benefit not?
  Hearken to the words of the Apostle.
"If the dead do not rise again,
  Why should we be baptized for the dead?"
What of the men of the family of Mattathias
  Who discharged their pious office of mercy?
As you have read, in that time of war?
  They atoned by their sacrifices for the sins
Of those who fell in the battle,
  And who had followed the way of the
  heathen.
Much more the Priests of the Son of God
  Shall avail to purify the dead,
By the sacrifices which they offer
  And by the prayers of their mouth.

Thirty-Day Novena of Meditations and Prayers

TYPICALLY, A NOVENA consists of acts of devotion performed on nine consecutive days to obtain a particular grace of either spiritual or temporal nature. Novenas also prepare the faithful for the great feasts of Our Lord, the Blessed Virgin Mary, and particular saints.

The first novena was made by the Blessed Virgin Mary and the apostles at the command of Our Lord himself. It lasted from the ascension of Christ into heaven until the descent of the Holy Spirit on the great feast of Pentecost, as Mary and the apostles waited in the Upper Room.

For anyone unfamiliar with a thirty-day "novena," it is recommended that you begin each day with the following prayer and then reflect on the passage for that day. Integrate the message of the individual reflections into some aspect of your daily life.

Prayer of
Blessed James Alberione

BLESSED SOULS, YOU are suffering and asking suffrage from me; I am in great danger and need, and I await aid and protection from you. So for this (month or year) I will offer all my prayers and especially all my good works for you. And you in turn remember my needs; deliver me from the dangers I face, and in particular, obtain for me this grace (mention petition). And let the first of you to enter heaven not cease to plead for me before the divine mercy until I, too, arrive there. May the Sacred Heart bless this agreement. Amen.

Day One
Praying for the Dead

"IN TRUTH we are guilty concerning our brother, in that we saw the distress of his soul, when he besought us and we would not listen; therefore is this distress come upon us."

— *GENESIS 42:21*

As the *Catechism of the Catholic Church* teaches:

The Church gives the name *Purgatory* to this final purification of the elect, which is entirely different from the punishment of the damned. The Church formulated her doctrine of faith on Purgatory especially at the Councils of Florence and Trent. The tradition of the Church, by reference to certain texts of Scripture, speaks of a cleansing fire.... This teaching is also based on the practice of prayer for the dead, already mentioned in Sacred Scripture: "Therefore, [Judas Maccabeus] made atonement for the dead, that they might be delivered from their sin" (2 Maccabees 12:45). From the beginning the Church has honored the memory of the dead and offered prayers in suffrage for them, above all the Eucharistic sacrifice, so that, thus purified, they may attain the beatific vision of God. The Church also commends almsgiving, indulgences, and works of penance undertaken on behalf of the dead [nos. 1031-1032].

Do all in your power to relieve and liberate these blessed souls. Remember the holy souls year-round. One traditional belief is that most souls are released on Christmas Day, not on All Souls' Day. By remembering the holy souls in your daily prayers during the summer months, you are giving them "Christmas in July." Pray the Stations of the Cross for the holy souls, especially during Lent. Do this novena for the holy souls prior to Our Lord's feast days and major Marian feast days. Offer Holy Mass for them once a month. The holy souls never rest. They suffer day and night.

And what becomes of all the merit of those Masses, and other suffrages, that are offered for souls which are not in purgatory? No prayer is ever wasted. Our Lord applies them to the souls as He sees fit.

GRACIOUSLY HEAR, O GOD, the fervent prayers we offer Thee for the suffering souls in purgatory, who, not having satisfied Thy justice, confide in Thine infinite mercy and our intercessions. Extend unto them Thy consolations, and redeem them, through Christ our Lord. Amen.

Eternal rest grant unto them, O Lord, and let perpetual light shine upon them. May they rest in peace. Amen.

"*I will without delay, immediately, come to the relief of the suffering souls in purgatory; with sobs and sighs I will invoke the Lord; with tears I will entreat Him; I will be their advocate by my prayers; I will especially offer up for them, or have offered for them, the Holy Sacrifice of the Mass and the prayers of the Rosary, in order that the Lord, with the eyes of His unspeakable mercy, may look down upon them, changing their desolation into comfort, their misery into joy, and their pains into everlasting glory and bliss.*"

— *ST. BERNARD*

Day Two
Benefits of Devotion to the Holy Souls

"KEEP YOURSELVES IN the love of God; wait for the mercy of our Lord Jesus Christ into eternal life."

— JUDE 1:21

THE SAINTS HAVE understood this devotion well throughout the history of the Church. There seems to be not a single chosen soul upon whom the Lord has not impressed His desire that every possible spiritual help be given to the souls of the departed.

This charity, issuing into a lifelong dedication to the souls in purgatory, dilates the heart with love for God, and for our neighbor on earth and in purgatory.

"Entirely centered in God, the love embodied in devotion to the holy souls purifies the affections of the mind and heart," writes Ladislaus Boros, S.J., in *Pain and Providence*. "[It confers] on its clients a most loving awareness of the nearness of the holy souls, the severity of their sufferings, the tremendous urgency for our prayers, the eloquence of their silence, the intensity of their love, the purity of their worship, the grandeur of their patience, the majesty of their gifts, and the greatness of their destiny. Our intercessions are never too late, even if we are praying decades after death, since God by His very nature knows no before and after. For God is all-present."

This devotion helps us see the holy souls through Our Lord's eyes, with His love, justice, and mercy. The love that inspires the apostolate of purgatory dares to imitate even the charity of God himself. It is filled with Jesus, with His Spirit, with His work, with His power, and with His victories.

Jesus is so grateful for the charity shown to His blessed souls that He cannot help anticipating for their helpers in this life a certain measure of the rewards of eternity.

Meditate today on the importance of the holy souls to Our Lord.

GRACIOUSLY HEAR, O GOD, the fervent prayers we offer Thee for the suffering souls in purgatory, who, not having satisfied Thy justice, confide in Thine infinite mercy and our intercessions. Extend unto them Thy consolations, and redeem them, through Christ our Lord. Amen.

Eternal rest grant unto them, O Lord, and let perpetual light shine upon them. May they rest in peace. Amen.

"It is charity that gives unity to all the virtues that make a man perfect."

— *ST. ALPHONSUS LIGUORI*

Day Three
The Mercy of God

"THE STEADFAST LOVE of the Lord never ceases, his mercies never come to an end."

— *LAMENTATIONS 3:22*

MOTHER MARY OF ST. AUSTIN writes in
The Divine Crucible of Purgatory:
"Likened unto Christ, the holy souls' suffering is not merely an expiation; it is also
an adoration. They offer their weakness in
homage to Omnipotence, their tears to
Beatitude, their poverty to Divine
Plentitude, their darkness to Light, their
silence to the Word, and their loneliness to
the ineffable happiness of the Trinity."
Theirs is a love that not only experiences
God's justice but also His "mercy." Their
love experiences Love that pardons, heals,
cherishes, elevates, and promises union.

Cardinal Allen offers this prayer: "Let us
bless God's name forever, that He has not
taken His mercy from us, that He has not
dealt with us according to our sins. Our
priests have offended, our princes have
offended, and our people have offended;
yet for His own Name's sake He has
looked upon us, and has kept us within
the household of salvation. Glory and

honor be to His holy name forevermore. Amen."

God's mercy is described as inconceivable, inexhaustible, an ocean without limit, and an abyss that is tender, infinite, and compassionate. Purgatory is a masterpiece of God's mercy.

How have you shown Christ's mercy today?

GRACIOUSLY HEAR, O GOD, the fervent prayers we offer Thee for the suffering souls in purgatory, who, not having satisfied Thy justice, confide in Thine infinite mercy and our intercessions. Extend unto them Thy consolations, and redeem them, through Christ our Lord. Amen.

Eternal rest grant unto them, O Lord, and let perpetual light shine upon them. May they rest in peace. Amen.

"*My mercy is greater than your sins and those of the entire world.... I let my Sacred Heart be pierced with a lance, thus opening wide the source of Mercy for you. Come, then, with trust to draw graces from this fountain. I never reject a contrite heart.*"

— *WORDS OF OUR LORD TO ST. FAUSTINA*

Day Four
Expiation of Sins

"BLESSED ARE THOSE who wash their robes, that they may have the right to the tree of life and that they may enter the city by the gates."

— *REVELATION 22:14*

"ALL WHO DIE in God's grace and friendship, but still imperfectly purified, are indeed assured of their eternal salvation; but after death they undergo purification, so as to achieve the holiness necessary to enter the joy of heaven" (*Catechism of the Catholic Church*, no. 1030).

The Right Rev. G. P. Dwyer says this about the holy souls:

> They no longer desire anything but God. And yet they cannot reach Him until their debt is paid. The sufferings of the holy souls spring from this double source — longing for God, the realization of sin.

> On earth we can turn to a hundred things to distract the mind, to muffle the cry of the heart. These escapes are denied the holy souls. Their focus is set on God and God alone! They see themselves as they really are. They see how

unfit they are to go to God. They see clearly their sins were an offense against God. They realize at last the malice of sin.

Redemptorists Maurice Becque and Louis Becque, in *Life After Death*, also write:

> These souls are waiting for God. They see Him better than they did on earth and are aspiring to contemplate Him in the full light of the beatific vision. They are happy at being saved, unhappy at being held back and having to delay. Freed from the burden of matter, they are ... *All to God, all in God, all for God.*

When you have confessed your sins, the guilt is removed. To remove the "stain," what charitable work will you take today?

GRACIOUSLY HEAR, O GOD, the fervent prayers we offer Thee for the suffering souls in purgatory, who, not having satisfied Thy justice, confide in Thine infinite mercy and our intercessions. Extend unto them Thy consolations, and redeem them, through Christ our Lord. Amen.

Eternal rest grant unto them, O Lord, and let perpetual light shine upon them. May they rest in peace. Amen.

"*By devotion to the holy souls, our progress in virtue and perfection is greatly hastened.*"

— *VENERABLE FRANCES OF THE BLESSED SACRAMENT*

Day Five
The Church Militant, Suffering, and Triumphant

"IF ONE MEMBER SUFFERS, all suffer together; if one member is honored, all rejoice together."

— *1 CORINTHIANS 12:26*

IN DAYS PAST, Trappist monks greeted one another with the words *Memento mori* ("Remember that you must die"). Death is the end merely of earthly life, but it is not the end of love. We are encouraged to make as many amends as possible in this life for the sins we have committed. Life is filled with suffering and sorrow, but Christians see in these things the love of a merciful God. It is the work of divine mercy that we are given the opportunity to do penance here on earth. Suffering comes to everyone.

Generous acceptance of all hardships in a spirit of penance — to accept every bereavement, illness, privation, as well as the wicked treatment of men, and every humiliation and difficult task, with humble hearts, for the intention of aiding the holy souls in purgatory — is all that is needed. If we use the treasures that are in our daily sufferings, we shall enrich ourselves with merits for eternity. We shall be the benefactors of the holy souls, and we shall prepare ourselves for entry into heaven.

GRACIOUSLY HEAR, O GOD, the fervent prayers we offer Thee for the suffering souls in purgatory, who, not having satisfied Thy justice, confide in Thine infinite mercy and our intercessions. Extend unto them Thy consolations, and redeem them, through Christ our Lord. Amen.

Eternal rest grant unto them, O Lord, and let perpetual light shine upon them. May they rest in peace. Amen.

"All that we offer to God in charity for the dead is changed into merit for ourselves, and we shall find it increased a hundredfold after our death."

— *ST. AMBROSE*

Day Six
Holy Abandonment

"HE wholly followed the LORD."

— *JOSHUA 14:14*

FATHER HUBERT writes in *The Mystery of Purgatory*:

Abandonment requires us to rest in Jesus in all the circumstances of our life, without exception, and it has its foundation in divine love. This love appeals to faith and confidence. The more perfectly we endeavor to practice abandonment, the more lovingly and freely we allow God's love to search out and purify, as by fire, the nooks and crannies of our self-love.

This life of abandonment is a kind of purgatory on earth and bears resemblance to life in the true purgatory. This expiatory rest in the midst of trials obtains eternal rest for the holy souls in purgatory.

By generously opening to the purifying and maturing influence of divine love in the restful purgatory of abandonment in this life, and by offering for the holy souls the sufferings experienced in that abandonment, we alleviate their pains and may by doing so avoid purgatory after our own death.

These silent sufferers plead with us to expiate their failures to rest in Our Lord during their lifetimes by us resting in Him now, in our own lives, through the practice of holy abandonment. The more generous our endeavors to rest in Jesus in the earthly purgatory of abandonment with the intention of helping the holy souls, the more efficacious becomes that sacred rest for them and for ourselves. The happy repose of abandonment through love purifies and matures our own souls, and it is a fitting expiation for the souls in purgatory.

Begin today to follow Our Lady. Abandon yourself to God!

GRACIOUSLY HEAR, O GOD, the fervent prayers we offer Thee for the suffering souls in purgatory, who, not having satisfied Thy justice, confide in Thine infinite mercy and our intercessions. Extend unto them Thy consolations, and redeem them, through Christ our Lord. Amen.

Eternal rest grant unto them, O Lord, and let perpetual light shine upon them. May they rest in peace. Amen.

"The soul's true life and repose are to abide in God."

— ST. ALBERT THE GREAT

Day Seven
Pain of Loss

"AND I WILL PUT this third into the fire,
and refine them as one refines silver, and
test them as gold is tested."

— *ZECHARIAH 13:9*

OH, THE SUFFERING of purgatory! We shall never know it, or understand it, until we are there. Yes, we cannot but think that the greatest, the keenest suffering of the soul will be the remembrance of that which it has seen for a passing moment, and the pining to behold again and forever the face of God. It has been revealed to saints that this desire is so intense that the soul would gladly place itself even in the most fearful tortures if it could thus become more quickly purged from that which holds it from the presence of God.

Once the soul sees the face of God even for one brief moment, the eyes of the soul can never close without inexpressible pain. To close them and shut out that vision is agony. Once the soul has left the body, it has but one desire: to unite itself to God, the only one worth loving, toward whom it is drawn, like a piece of iron by a powerful magnet.

Now the soul realizes the utter beauty and lovableness of God, how good God is, and what joy it is to be with Him. The divine attributes — goodness, holiness, love, wisdom — are meaningful to the soul as never before. It is as if the ardor of God's own love had set the soul aflame with adoration, gratitude, and love. The soul sees clearly how Providence designed all things — both the visible and invisible universe and the supernatural world — so that men could come to know and love God. It pants, "God! God! I must be with God!" as its constant cry!

St. Teresa of Ávila received but a passing glimpse of the hand of our Blessed Lord and went into ecstasy. St. Francis heard an angel give one touch of a violin, and the saint nearly died of pleasure. The mind of man cannot comprehend eternity.

Pope John Paul II encourages us to go out into nature. There you will meet God the Creator, and it will help open your heart to the love of God.

GRACIOUSLY HEAR, O GOD, the fervent prayers we offer Thee for the suffering souls in purgatory, who, not having satisfied Thy justice, confide in Thine infinite mercy and our intercessions. Extend unto them Thy consolations, and redeem them, through Christ our Lord. Amen.

Eternal rest grant unto them, O Lord, and let perpetual light shine upon them. May they rest in peace. Amen.

"The pain of loss is the greatest pain of all the pains of purgatory."

— *ST. JOHN CHRYSOSTOM*

Day Eight
Pain of the Senses

"IT IS APPOINTED for men to die once,
and after that comes judgment."

— HEBREWS 9:27

THE SUFFERING OF the holy souls is worse than any illness or suffering on earth.

They suffer the pain of loss; they suffer the pain of sorrow for their sins; and they suffer the pain of helplessness and desolation because they are unable to help themselves. They suffer the pain of desire, of being on fire for the love of God. They suffer the pain of not knowing when they will enter heaven.

The soul sees what God intended it to be; the beauty and the strength that God meant it to have; the place God intended for it in His plan of salvation for the entire world.

And the soul sees what obstacles it erected — its selfishness, its cowardice, its shallow satisfactions, its perversions of God's graces and His gifts. All these came between God and the soul in life.

The holy souls beg us for our prayers and sacrifices!

St. Patrick's Purgatory on Station Island in Ireland has long been renowned as a place of penance and pilgrimage. Even today, barefoot pilgrims travel to Lough Derg in summer months and spend three days praying, fasting, and following the Stations of the Cross within the ninth-century cells.

What island do you use to pray and fast?

GRACIOUSLY HEAR, O GOD, the fervent prayers we offer Thee for the suffering souls in purgatory, who, not having satisfied Thy justice, confide in Thine infinite mercy and our intercessions. Extend unto them Thy consolations, and redeem them, through Christ our Lord. Amen.

Eternal rest grant unto them, O Lord, and let perpetual light shine upon them. May they rest in peace. Amen.

"*If a ray of heavenly light could draw aside the veil from your eyes, you would see these suffering souls hovering around each station with upraised arms imploring you, 'Have pity on me, have pity on me! In pity for us, make the Way of the Cross for me, your father, your mother, your friend.'* "

— *ST. LEONARD OF PORT MAURICE*

✠

*D*ay Nine
Conformity to God's Will

"ABBA, FATHER, all things are possible
to thee; remove this cup from me; yet not
what I will, but what thou wilt."

— MARK 14:36

THE GREATEST SANCTITY on earth below, or in heaven above, is conformity to the will of God.

The souls in purgatory are entirely conformed to the will of God; therefore, they correspond with His goodness, are contented with all He ordains, and are entirely purified from the guilt of their sins. They are purified from sin because in this life they have abhorred sins and confessed them with true contrition; and for this reason God remits their guilt, so that only the stains of sin remain, and these must be devoured by the fire. Thus freed from guilt and united to the will of God, they see Him clearly according to that degree of light which He allows them, and they comprehend how great a good is the fruition of God, for which all souls were created.

Their zeal for appeasing God's justice is so great that not only do they not decline to suffer, but they would also consent to their very annihilation for the greater glory of God; for God's will is their will. They praise God's justice, and their suffering is voluntary and loving. We must do God's will on earth. This is how we can avoid purgatory.

What have you done to accept your sorrows?

GRACIOUSLY HEAR, O GOD, the fervent prayers we offer Thee for the suffering souls in purgatory, who, not having satisfied Thy justice, confide in Thine infinite mercy and our intercessions. Extend unto them Thy consolations, and redeem them, through Christ our Lord. Amen.

Eternal rest grant unto them, O Lord, and let perpetual light shine upon them. May they rest in peace. Amen.

"God's will — nothing more, nothing less, nothing else."

— *ST. ELIZABETH ANN SETON*

Day Ten
Languishing for God's Love

"DID NOT OUR hearts burn within us
while he talked to us on the road."

— *LUKE 24:32*

WHAT IS THIS mysterious fire? Martin Jugie, an Augustinian of the Assumption, replies, "Is it not the very fire of love, burning in the depths of the soul, while the soul, drawn irresistibly toward its Well-beloved, can neither reach nor see Him?"

Stopped in its progress by an insurmountable obstacle, that love becomes a fire, a burning sorrow, a kind of spiritual fever, which cannot be adequately expressed by the human word *fire*. The holy souls burn "interiorly" for God. Their hearts are on fire for God.

Hebrews 12:29 teaches that "our God is a consuming fire." God burns for love of us. God loves us more than anybody else and more than anybody can. In the words of St. Catherine of Siena: "Our very nature is fire, created in the fire of His love. He is the fire, and we are the sparks."

For love is like fire, which ever rises upward

with the desire to be absorbed in the center of its sphere. Here is the burning desire and longing for God that far surpasses the heat of any earthly fire. Thus, we rightly speak of the fire of purgatory and of the cleansing flames. But they are flames of love. Love itself is the fire that attacks and devours the impurities of the soul. And so, the holy souls willingly suffer the agony of love.

St. Gregory the Great, speaking of purgatory, calls it "a penitential fire harder to endure than all the tribulations of this world." St. Augustine says that the torment of fire alone endured by the holy souls in purgatory exceeds all the tortures inflicted on the martyrs.

Everything you do, do with love, today and always.

GRACIOUSLY HEAR, O GOD, the fervent prayers we offer Thee for the suffering souls in purgatory, who, not having satisfied Thy justice, confide in Thine infinite mercy and our intercessions. Extend unto them Thy consolations, and redeem them, through Christ our Lord. Amen.

Eternal rest grant unto them, O Lord, and let perpetual light shine upon them. May they rest in peace. Amen.

"I will pray to You that You may give me holiness, and to all the living and dead, pardon, that someday we may all be together with You, our dearest God."

— *ST. JOHN NEUMANN*

Day Eleven
Duration of Purgatory

"IF I HAVE FOUND favor in your sight, O
king, and if it please the king, let my life be
given me at my petition, and my people at
my request."

— ESTHER 7:3

AT FÁTIMA IN 1917, the Blessed Virgin Mary appeared to three shepherd children: Lucia, Blessed Jacinta, and Blessed Francesco. Shortly before the apparitions took place, a young girl about fourteen years old died in the village. The children asked Our Lady whether she had been saved. The Blessed Virgin advised them that the girl had been saved but would be in purgatory until the end of the world. As a result of this revelation, many prayers were offered up for her soul.

This poignantly reminds us of the existence of purgatory, the length of time souls must remain there, and the tremendous importance of praying for the suffering souls. St. Augustine teaches that the duration of purification in purgatory for a soul is fixed according to the measure of sin and penance of each individual. The duration may be measured by days, and yet, because of the intensity of pain, it may seem longer.

Brother Constantine of the Redeemer appeared after his death and said, "I suffered three days, and they seemed to me to have been three thousand years."

Pray, pray, pray!

GRACIOUSLY HEAR, O GOD, the fervent prayers we offer Thee for the suffering souls in purgatory, who, not having satisfied Thy justice, confide in Thine infinite mercy and our intercessions. Extend unto them Thy consolations, and redeem them, through Christ our Lord. Amen.

Eternal rest grant unto them, O Lord, and let perpetual light shine upon them. May they rest in peace. Amen.

"Some souls would suffer in purgatory until the Day of Judgment if they were not relieved by the prayers of the Church."

— ST. ROBERT BELLARMINE

Day Twelve
Duty, Power, and Privilege

"THE GUESTS IN my house have forgotten me; my maidservants count me as a stranger; I have become an alien in their eyes."

— JOB 19:15

LIKE JOB, THE HOLY SOULS in purgatory feel completely abandoned.

Charity and gratitude not only demand that we pray for the souls in purgatory, but it is also for us a positive duty, which we, in God's justice, are bound to fulfill. God has given us the power and privilege to deliver the holy souls from purgatory. Nothing pleases God more than praying for the holy souls. God is more pleased with us if we pay our debts here on earth because of His paternal desire to receive us without delay into His home.

We must pray for all of the souls in purgatory in general, and in a special manner for the souls of our parents, friends, and benefactors, as well as for others who have a right to our grateful remembrance.

Perhaps some of these poor souls are suffering on our account. Perhaps they are relatives or friends who have loved us too much, or who have been induced to commit sins by our words or example. Perhaps we owe these blessed souls our gratitude for the priest who baptized us or gave us our First Communion, or for a speaker or preacher who inspired us. God places His rights and gifts into our hands, and therefore our responsibility is great if we hold the ransom in hand without using it.

We tend to "canonize" our clergy and loved ones immediately after their death. Father Frederick Faber tells us, "We are apt to leave off too soon praying for our parents, friends, or relatives, imagining with a foolish and unenlightened esteem for the holiness of their lives, that they are freed from purgatory much sooner than they really are."

Let us offer a very great part of our suffrages for these unknown forgotten souls, and in a special way for priests, consecrated religious, and nonbelievers.

GRACIOUSLY HEAR, O GOD, the fervent prayers we offer Thee for the suffering souls in purgatory, who, not having satisfied Thy justice, confide in Thine infinite mercy and our intercessions. Extend unto them Thy consolations, and redeem them, through Christ our Lord. Amen.

Eternal rest grant unto them, O Lord, and let perpetual light shine upon them. May they rest in peace. Amen.

"If we were thoroughly convinced of the torments of purgatory, could we then so easily forget our parents? ... If God would permit them to show themselves, we would see them cast themselves down at our feet. 'My children,' they would cry out, 'have mercy on us! Oh, do not forsake us!' "

— ST. JOHN VIANNEY

Day Thirteen
Empty Reminiscences

"SHE WAS FULL of good works and acts of charity."

— ACTS 9:36

IF ONLY THE dead could speak from their graves, they would cry out and say: "All these monuments, and this worldly pageantry only crush us. They only satisfy the vanity of the living, but in no way alleviate our sufferings in purgatory." They would ask:

Give us your feet by going to hear Mass for us.

Give us your eyes by watching for opportunities to perform good deeds for us.

Give us your hands by giving alms or an offering for a Mass.

Give us your lips by praying for us.

Give us your tongue by encouraging others to be charitable to us.

Give us your memory by remembering us in your devotions.

Give us your body by offering up to God all its labors, fatigues, and penances for us.

GRACIOUSLY HEAR, O GOD, the fervent prayers we offer Thee for the suffering souls in purgatory, who, not having satisfied Thy justice, confide in Thine infinite mercy and our intercessions. Extend unto them Thy consolations, and redeem them, through Christ our Lord. Amen.

Eternal rest grant unto them, O Lord, and let perpetual light shine upon them. May they rest in peace. Amen.

"*Our dead are among the invisible, not among the absent.*"

— *BLESSED POPE JOHN XXIII*

Day Fourteen
Special Duty of Children

"WHOEVER HONORS HIS father atones for sins, and whoever glorifies his mother is like one who lays up treasure."

— *SIRACH 3:3-4*

PARENTS, GRANDPARENTS, AND GUARDIANS: Form kind and merciful hearts in your children and grandchildren. You will have planted the seed of reverence, and in due time this will manifest itself and will assure you of their suffrages. Bring the children to the cemetery, teach them prayers and how to "offer up" little things for the suffering souls. During the July 13, 1917, apparition of Fátima, Our Lady taught this prayer to the children to be said when they would have some sacrifice to offer God:

Sacrifice Prayer

O MY JESUS, it is for love of Thee, in reparation for the offenses committed against the Immaculate Heart of Mary, and for the conversion of poor sinners.

Instruct children to pray and sacrifice for departed loved ones. Instruct them especially by your own example.

GRACIOUSLY HEAR, O GOD, the fervent prayers we offer Thee for the suffering souls in purgatory, who, not having satisfied Thy justice, confide in Thine infinite mercy and our intercessions. Extend unto them Thy consolations, and redeem them, through Christ our Lord. Amen.

Eternal rest grant unto them, O Lord, and let perpetual light shine upon them. May they rest in peace. Amen.

"*We reckon Paradise to be our home.... There are a great many of those we love waiting for us there — father, and mother, and brothers, and children, there in great company they await us.... Oh, when we come to see them and to embrace them, what gladness will it be both for us and for them!*"

— *ST. CYPRIAN*

Day Fifteen
State of Grace

"OFFER SPIRITUAL sacrifices acceptable to God through Jesus Christ."

— *1 PETER 2:5*

ANY GOOD WORK for the holy souls must be carried out in a state of grace in order for the holy souls to benefit from it. When the soul is in a state of mortal sin, it cannot make satisfaction either for itself or for others. Prayer from a soul in grace moves God and is, as St. Augustine says, "a key to heaven."

When there is an indulgence, it is good to have the intention of applying it to the holy souls in general, or to a particular soul, or to a category of souls — for example, the most abandoned souls, souls closest to heaven, or deceased consecrated to God (clergy and Religious).

The souls in purgatory are unspeakably holy. They died in the state of grace. They can no longer sin. They are free from sin and temptation. However, they are called "poor" because their poverty is the loss of the sight of God. They are poor because they cannot help themselves. Their time of merit is over. They are poor because their voices are silent and are unable to speak to us. They plead for our Masses, Rosaries, and Stations of the Cross.

St. Pompilius Pirrotti had a great devotion to the poor souls. When he prayed the Rosary, the holy souls prayed along with him, shouting in response to each Hail Mary recited. The souls in purgatory were tranquil and full of joy while the Rosary was prayed.

St. Joseph Cafasso was called a "glutton" for indulgences, as a means for both avoiding purgatory himself and for helping the souls in purgatory speedily attain heaven. We, too, must be greedy for grace for the holy souls. Let us pray that we will live and die in the state of grace.

Have you become a "glutton" for spiritual sacrifices?

GRACIOUSLY HEAR, O GOD, the fervent prayers we offer Thee for the suffering souls in purgatory, who, not having satisfied Thy justice, confide in Thine infinite mercy and our intercessions. Extend unto them Thy consolations, and redeem them, through Christ our Lord. Amen.

Eternal rest grant unto them, O Lord, and let perpetual light shine upon them. May they rest in peace. Amen.

"The heart of a helper, so close to purgatory, must always be on fire."

— BLESSED MARY OF PROVIDENCE, FOUNDRESS OF THE HOLY SOULS HELPERS

Day Sixteen
Source of Joy and Peace

"NOW I REJOICE in my sufferings for your sake, and in my flesh I complete what is lacking in Christ's afflictions for the sake of his body, that is, the church."

— COLOSSIANS 1:24

THE FIRST AND GREATEST consolation of the pains of purgatory is the absolute certainty of salvation, which sweetens the most intense pains of purgatory. However, the holy souls must atone for their sins. St. Catherine of Genoa tells us: "It is true that the overflowing love of God bestows upon the souls in purgatory a happiness beyond expression; this happiness does not in the least diminish the pain. In this manner the holy souls at the same time experience the greatest happiness, and the most excessive pain; and the one does not prevent the other."

St. Gertrude states that the soul knowing the will of God and seeing its stains of sin would choose the pains of purgatory rather than ascend straight to heaven, even if it had the choice.

Have no fear of purgatory. Welcome the opportunity to be in union with God.

GRACIOUSLY HEAR, O GOD, the fervent
prayers we offer Thee for the suffering
souls in purgatory, who, not having satisfied
Thy justice, confide in Thine infinite mercy
and our intercessions. Extend unto them
Thy consolations, and redeem them,
through Christ our Lord. Amen.

Eternal rest grant unto them, O Lord, and
let perpetual light shine upon them. May
they rest in peace. Amen.

*"The more the soul loves, the more it
desires to love, and the greater its suffering, the
greater its healing."*

— *ST. COLUMBAN*

Day *Seventeen*
Intercessory Prayer

"TRULY, TRULY, I say to you, if you ask anything of the Father, he will give it to you in my name."

— JOHN 16:23

IN ROME, there is a church called Sacro Cuore del Suffragio (Sacred Heart of Suffrages). It was built in the late nineteenth century. At that time, the priest wanted to name the church after the holy souls, but that was not to be. Unusual occurrences related to the holy souls were reported to the priest in charge, and he began collecting relics and evidence of the holy souls in a small museum inside the church. Each of these relics of evidence had a story. Every story had three recurring themes: (1) there was proof that purgatory exists; (2) every relic in some way, when touched by a holy soul, was scorched; and (3) the holy souls were in desperate need of Masses.

The prayers of intercession and petition that the Church never ceases to raise to God have great value. They are "characteristic of a heart attuned to God's mercy" (*Catechism of the Catholic Church*, no. 2635).

The Lord always lets himself be moved by His children's supplications, for He is the God of the living.

Have you created a special place in your heart for the suffering souls?

GRACIOUSLY HEAR, O GOD, the fervent prayers we offer Thee for the suffering souls in purgatory, who, not having satisfied Thy justice, confide in Thine infinite mercy and our intercessions. Extend unto them Thy consolations, and redeem them, through Christ our Lord. Amen.

Eternal rest grant unto them, O Lord, and let perpetual light shine upon them. May they rest in peace. Amen.

"If a soul is delivered by prayer from purgatory I accept it as if I had myself been delivered from captivity, and I will assuredly reward it according to the abundance of my mercy."

— *WORDS OF OUR LORD TO ST. GERTRUDE*

Day Eighteen
Offerings of Light

"AND YOU SHALL command the people of Israel that they bring to you pure beaten olive oil for the light, that a lamp may be set up to burn continually."

— *EXODUS 27:20*

Lights have always played an important role in the history of the Church. Lighted candles have been part of the Mass and other liturgies since the early days of Christianity, and they were kept burning for periods of time at the tombs of martyrs, as a sign of remembrance.

During the Middle Ages, offerings were made for maintaining lamps that were kept burning on the graves throughout the year, which served to comfort the souls of the departed. The burning lamps or candles signified Christ, the eternal Light, whom we implore in our prayers to shine upon the departed. These lights were called "Dead Lights" or "All Souls Lights."

The candles kept a silent vigil and so came to be known as "vigil lights." The offering of a lighted candle is a praiseworthy prayer in action for the holy souls languishing in purgatory.

GRACIOUSLY HEAR, O GOD, the fervent prayers we offer Thee for the suffering souls in purgatory, who, not having satisfied Thy justice, confide in Thine infinite mercy and our intercessions. Extend unto them Thy consolations, and redeem them, through Christ our Lord. Amen.

Eternal rest grant unto them, O Lord, and let perpetual light shine upon them. May they rest in peace. Amen.

"Though the deceased is buried in the earth, thou must not omit to burn oil and wax on his grave, for this is pleasing to God and merits great reward."

— *ST. ATHANASIUS*

Day Nineteen
The Holy Mass

"HOW LOVELY IS thy dwelling place,
O LORD of Hosts!"

— *PSALM: 84:1*

ST. AUGUSTINE and his brother, Navigius, stood beside their dying mother, Monica. Navigius wished that his mother could die on their native soil and not in a strange land. But the dying St. Monica said: "Bury my body wherever you please. Take no thought about that. Only one thing I beg of you. That at the Lord's altar, wherever you may be, remember me."

If only this were the first thing to occur to us in connection with our dead, to remember them at God's altar. The Holy Sacrifice of the Mass is the most efficacious means to help, to relieve, and to deliver the souls in purgatory.

The Church has always remembered the dead in the Holy Sacrifice of the Mass and exhorted the faithful to pray for them. Holy Mother Church urges us to pray for the souls in purgatory. Although they cannot help themselves, these poor souls do have recourse to our prayers. It is said that in time of affliction we know our true friends. But what affliction could be compared to theirs?

Be moved with compassion. Make their desire your desire: to behold the face of God, to possess Him, to love Him, and to praise Him with the angels forever in heaven.

St. Anselm reminds us that "a single Mass offered for oneself during life may be worth more than a thousand celebrated for the same intention after death." The Mass heals the living and the dead.

Whom do you miss the most? Whom do you wish you could have done more for? Who are your enemies? Have a Mass offered for them! And remember to have a Mass offered for yourself.

As Michael Brown suggests in *Afterlife*:

Begin a life novena: a Mass offered for each year of your life where you can meditate on a different year each day. During each Mass ask God to send love and blessings where you have failed to love and to bless every person who came anywhere near your presence, from the moment of your conception to the present. Then you can begin the necessary purification here on earth.

GRACIOUSLY HEAR, O GOD, The fervent prayers we offer Thee for the suffering souls in purgatory, who, not having satisfied Thy justice, confide in Thine infinite mercy and our intercessions. Extend unto them Thy consolations, and redeem them, through Christ our Lord. Amen.

Eternal rest grant unto them, O Lord, and let perpetual light shine upon them. May they rest in peace. Amen.

"Let the love and compassion for your neighbor lead you to the holy table; for nothing is so well calculated to obtain eternal rest for the holy souls."

— *ST. BONAVENTURE*

Day Twenty
Holy Communion and Adoration

"I HAVE LOVED YOU with an everlasting love."

— *JEREMIAH 31:3*

CAN WE REMAIN inactive for the holy souls? We can help the suffering souls so easily. They are poor and we are rich. They can do nothing for themselves; we can do everything for them. They can no longer assist at Mass and cleanse themselves in the Blood of Christ. We can offer the sacrifice and Christ's precious Blood for them. They can no longer eat the bread of life. We can receive it for them in Holy Communion.

Heed their voiceless pleadings. And on the day of your judgment, Jesus will say to you, "Come, O blessed of my Father.... I was in prison and you came to me" (Matthew 25:34, 36).

Eucharistic Adoration is one of the most powerful forms of prayer in assisting the holy souls reach heaven. Eucharistic Adoration is intercessory prayer. The adorers assume the office of mediators on behalf of mankind by their unceasing prayers, offering up supplications day and night to

God's throne of mercy on behalf of the members of the Church Suffering.

Our intercessory prayers give the suffering souls great comfort and relief. From the Sacred Host, streams of alleviating grace flow into the expiatory realms of purgatory, bringing unspeakable relief to those imprisoned there.

Offer heartfelt prayers before the Blessed Sacrament on behalf of the suffering souls.

GRACIOUSLY HEAR, O GOD, the fervent prayers we offer Thee for the suffering souls in purgatory, who, not having satisfied Thy justice, confide in Thine infinite mercy and our intercessions. Extend unto them Thy consolations, and redeem them, through Christ our Lord. Amen.

Eternal rest grant unto them, O Lord, and let perpetual light shine upon them. May they rest in peace. Amen.

"Behold the Lamb of God, behold God himself. Adore him!"

— *ST. PETER JULIAN EYMARD*

Day Twenty-One
Love of the Blessed Mother

"THEN SHE SAID, 'I have one small request to make of you; do not refuse me.' And the king said to her, 'Make your request, my mother; for I will not refuse you.' "

— *1 KINGS 2:20*

EXCEPT FOR THE MASS, there is no prayer so powerful for the release of souls from purgatory as the Rosary. The Virgin Mary told St. Dominic that the release of the souls in purgatory is one of the chief effects of the Rosary.

The Blessed Virgin offers our prayers to God. She embellishes them. Divinely skillful, she knows how to make gold of our dross, our impurities. The prayer, even when made with little attention, is always a prayer, and our Blessed Mother supplies that which it lacks. She is ceaselessly busy in covering our weaknesses before the face of God.

Our Lady said to St. Bridget: "I am the Mother of the souls in purgatory. Their torments are continually eased in some manner through my intercession. For it pleases the Lord to remit in this manner some punishments which are theirs due by justice."

A beautiful legend says that when Jesus was bleeding to death on the cross, an angel asked Him to whom the last drop of His heart's blood should belong, and He answered: "To my beloved Mother, that she may the more easily endure her sorrow." "Not so, my Son," Mary is said to have answered. "Grant it to the souls in purgatory, that they may be free from pain on at least one day of the year."

St. Alphonsus Liguori and Pope Pius XII encouraged us to wear the Brown Scapular of the Blessed Virgin as a sign of consecration to Mary's Immaculate Heart. Archbishop Fulton Sheen said, "If you are devoted to Our Lady, you will never lose your soul."

Swap with Our Lady. Pray for *her* intentions and give her *your* intentions.

GRACIOUSLY HEAR, O GOD, the fervent prayers we offer Thee for the suffering souls in purgatory, who, not having satisfied Thy justice, confide in Thine infinite mercy and our intercessions. Extend unto them Thy consolations, and redeem them, through Christ our Lord. Amen.

Eternal rest grant unto them, O Lord, and let perpetual light shine upon them. May they rest in peace. Amen.

"To Mary was given the power, by her intercession and merits, to release the souls from purgatory, particularly those that were foremost in their devotion to her."

— *ST. BERNARDINE OF SIENA*

Day Twenty-Two
Guardian Angels

"BEHOLD, I send an angel before you, to guard you on the way and to bring you to the place which I have prepared."

— *EXODUS 23:20*

OUT OF GOD'S excess of goodness
and love He has given His angels charge
over us.

Our guardian angels have the specific mis-
sion of helping every person in their charge
to reach heaven. Burning with the love of
God and full of intense love for us, our
angels devote all their glorious intelligence
and knowledge, all their power and vigi-
lance, to protect and defend us. Our angels
are interceding and praying constantly for
us with incredible fervor to God, before the
throne of the Most High.

The Doctors of the Church teach that the
guardianship of the holy angels over the
souls of men only terminate at the soul's
entrance into heaven. The guardian angel
conducts the soul to the place of expiation
and remains there with it to console and
encourage it, and to inspire its friends on
earth with desires and good works for its
speedy delivery into Paradise.

The angels reveal to the poor souls those who are assisting them by their prayers. When the hour of release has struck for the suffering soul, the guardian angel, with the speed of lightning, leads the soul to heaven. The guardian angel is often accompanied by a multitude of angels, so the entrance of the soul into heaven is truly a triumphant one!

Invoke the assistance of your guardian angel on behalf of your departed loved ones, and recommend them to his powerful intercession during Mass. Venerate your guardian angel, because he is always in God's presence, contemplating Him and praying for you with great love. And remember that he is forever at your side.

GRACIOUSLY HEAR, O GOD, the fervent prayers we offer Thee for the suffering souls in purgatory, who, not having satisfied Thy justice, confide in Thine infinite mercy and our intercessions. Extend unto them Thy consolations, and redeem them, through Christ our Lord. Amen.

Eternal rest grant unto them, O Lord, and let perpetual light shine upon them. May they rest in peace. Amen.

"Have confidence in your guardian angel. Treat him as a lifelong friend — that is what he is — and he will render you a thousand services in the ordinary affairs of each day."

— *ST. JOSEMARÍA ESCRIVÁ*

Day Twenty-Three
Avoiding Purgatory

"WHOEVER BRINGS BACK a sinner
from the error of his way will save his soul
from death."

— JAMES 5:20

YES, WE ARE GIVEN the grace to avoid purgatory! Do all in your power to help the holy souls! Accept God's holy will. Avoid sin at all cost. All sin is despicable to God. Forgive. Perform acts of kindness. Implore God to grant you to be holy and happy. Let us be faithful to our duties in life. Pray to St. Joseph for a happy death. Remember to pray for the dying. They become the holy souls! Consider monthly confession, daily Mass, and the reading of Sacred Scripture every day. The more you pray for the holy souls, the higher your level in purgatory will be — or perhaps you will avoid purgatory altogether!

St. Ambrose observes that God loves to be forced, and that they who pursue Him most, and with the greatest intensity, are the men and women He makes the most of. Imitate the good thief: Snatch heaven out of God's hands. Steal away His Paradise. Do something worthy of Him, worthy of yourself, and worthy of Paradise. If no better means occur to you, at least strive to be greatly concerned for the poor souls in pur-gatory.

GRACIOUSLY HEAR, O GOD, the fervent prayers we offer Thee for the suffering souls in purgatory, who, not having satisfied Thy justice, confide in Thine infinite mercy and our intercessions. Extend unto them Thy consolations, and redeem them, through Christ our Lord. Amen.

Eternal rest grant unto them, O Lord, and let perpetual light shine upon them. May they rest in peace. Amen.

"There is a need of living well, but there is even more need of dying well. A good death is everything."

— *BLESSED LOUIS GUANELLA*

Day Twenty-Four
Almsgiving

"FOR ALMSGIVING DELIVERS from death,
and it will purge away every sin."

— TOBIT 12:9

THERE IS ABUNDANT proof in Scripture of the efficacy of giving alms for the benefit of the souls in purgatory. Judas Maccabeus, having lost a great number of warriors in battle, ordered a collection to be made and sent the proceeds to Jerusalem to have sacrifice offered for the deceased.

God does not so much regard the amount of alms given as He does the heart of the one who gives. To remove a scandal, to repair an injury, to pay debts — in a word, to make good whatever the departed souls failed to settle before leaving this world — all of these are meritorious works by which the term in purgatory may be shortened.

It is better, says St. John Chrysostom, to give alms to the poor than to work a miracle or to raise a dead man; for in working a miracle you are beholden to God, but in giving alms God is beholden to you. And therefore, the saint explains, since God is indebted to you, then tell Him plainly you will be paid with no other coin but that of Paradise. If He thinks of sending you to purgatory, tell Him you will be first paid what He is pleased to owe you, because He has promised you life everlasting. And therefore, let Him first place you in Paradise, and you will have leisure to talk of purgatory.

St. John of God collected alms for his hospital in the streets of Granada. He called out, "Give alms, my brothers and sisters, for the love and mercy of yourselves." He did not say, "Pity the poor sick!" He said, "Be merciful to yourselves!"

Consider how you share your goods with others. The benefits flow both ways.

GRACIOUSLY HEAR, O GOD, the fervent
prayers we offer Thee for the suffering
souls in purgatory, who, not having satisfied
Thy justice, confide in Thine infinite mercy
and our intercessions. Extend unto them
Thy consolations, and redeem them,
through Christ our Lord. Amen.

Eternal rest grant unto them, O Lord, and
let perpetual light shine upon them. May
they rest in peace. Amen.

"He who purifies himself from his faults in the present satisfies with a penny a debt of a thousand silver pieces; and he who waits until the other life to pay his debts consents to pay a thousand silver pieces for that which he might have paid before with a penny."

— *ST. CATHERINE OF GENOA*

Day Twenty-Five
Works of Penance

"AND EVERY MAN of Israel cried out to God with great fervor, and they humbled themselves with much fasting."

— JUDITH 4:9

SCRIPTURE SHOWS US that prayer and fasting for the dead existed among the people of the earliest centuries. On the death of Joseph's father, Jacob, there was a period of mourning lasting seventy days. On the announcement of the death of Saul, all the inhabitants of Jabesh imposed upon themselves a seven-day fast. These practices were not only expressions of mourning but also suffrages for the dead.

The word *fasting* comes from a Hebrew word that means "to cover or shut one's mouth." The Greek word means "not to eat." Prayer and fasting can bring about change or relief even in the most critical situations. Fasting goes beyond the realm of food and into our actions and thoughts.

We allow God to use fasting to move us forward on our way of holiness. Fasting is an important dimension of this growth. It purifies our heart in order to open it wide to God and to our neighbor.

We are all called to fast. However, not all are called to fast in the same way. We should seek God, ask His direction, and then follow the impulses we sense coming from Him:

Fast from bitterness — feast on forgiveness.

Fast from self-concern — feast on compassion for others.

Fast from personal anxiety — feast on eternal truth.

Fast from anger — feast on patience.

Fast from words that destroy — feast on words that build.

Fast from discontent — feast on gratitude.

Fast from discouragement — feast on hope.

GRACIOUSLY HEAR, O GOD, the fervent prayers we offer Thee for the suffering souls in purgatory, who, not having satisfied Thy justice, confide in Thine infinite mercy and our intercessions. Extend unto them Thy consolations, and redeem them, through Christ our Lord. Amen.

Eternal rest grant unto them, O Lord, and let perpetual light shine upon them. May they rest in peace. Amen.

"Let us strive to do penance in this life. How sweet will be the death of those who have done penance for all their sins and need not go to purgatory!"

— *ST. TERESA OF ÁVILA*

Day Twenty-Six
Good Works

"THE FRUIT OF the Spirit is love, joy, peace, patience, kindness, goodness, faithfulness, gentleness, self-control."

— *GALATIANS 5:22-23*

ST. FRANCIS DE SALES was accustomed to saying that we practice all the corporal works of mercy together when we assist the suffering souls:

> Is it not in some manner, to visit the sick, to obtain by our prayers the relief of the poor suffering souls in purgatory?

> Is it not to give drink to those who thirst after the vision of God, and who are enveloped in burning flames, to share with them the dew of our prayers?

> Is it not to feed the hungry, to aid in their deliverance by the means which faith suggests?

> Is it not truly to ransom prisoners?

> Is it not truly to clothe the naked, to procure for them a garment of light, a raiment of glory?

Is it not an admirable degree of hospitality, to procure their admission into the heavenly Jerusalem, and to make them fellow citizens with the saints and domestics of God?

Is it not a greater service to place souls in heaven than to bury bodies in the earth?

As to [the spiritual works of mercy], is it not a work whose merit may be compared to that of counseling the weak, correcting the wayward, instructing the ignorant, forgiving offenses, enduring injuries?

And what consolation, however great, that can be given to the afflicted of this world is comparable with that which is brought by our prayers to those poor souls which have such bitter need of them?

GRACIOUSLY HEAR, O GOD, the fervent
prayers we offer Thee for the suffering
souls in purgatory, who, not having satisfied
Thy justice, confide in Thine infinite mercy
and our intercessions. Extend unto them
Thy consolations, and redeem them,
through Christ our Lord. Amen.

Eternal rest grant unto them, O Lord, and
let perpetual light shine upon them. May
they rest in peace. Amen.

"*Ah! How many poor souls are left to
suffer in consequences of lukewarmness, want of
zeal for God's glory, and the salvation of their
neighbor!*"

— *BLESSED ANNE CATHERINE EMMERICH*

Day Twenty-Seven
Gratitude

"I THANK MY GOD in all my remembrance of you, always in every prayer of mine for you all making my prayer with joy."

— PHILIPPIANS 1:3

THE SOULS IN PURGATORY do not wait until they have entered heaven to repay our kindness to them. By their prayers, they shield their friends from danger and protect them from the evils that threaten them. They will help you during times of temptation, as well as during times of trial and anguish. Be assured that they stand ready to help you.

What consolation it will be to know that we abbreviated their sufferings! How great will their gratitude be after their deliverance! They will manifest it by praying for us, and obtaining for us the help that is so necessary in this valley of tears. In prosperity, people forget those who have helped them in adversity. But it will not be so with the souls in purgatory.

After being admitted to the kingdom of heaven through the help of our prayers, "they will solicit," says St. Bernard, "the most precious gifts of grace on our behalf, and because the merciful shall obtain mercy, we will receive after our death the reward of whatever may have been done for the souls in purgatory during our life." He adds, "Others will pray for us, and we shall share more abundantly in the suffrages which the Church offers without ceasing, for those who sleep in the Lord."

To do good to the inhabitants of purgatory is a sure means of winning their gratitude. They pray for us with such an intensity, and a fervor so great, that God can refuse them nothing. Their first act when they reach heaven is to pray before the throne of God unceasingly for us until we arrive safely home in heaven.

St. Gertrude offered all her merits for the dead. She said to Our Lord, "I hope, O Lord, that Thou wilt frequently cast the eyes of Thy mercy on my indigence." He replied, "What can I do more for one who has thus deprived herself of all things through charity than to cover her immediately with charity? And now, what advantages have you, who are seated on the shore of an ocean, over those who sit by a little rivulet?"

Those who keep their good works for themselves have the rivulet. But those who renounce them in love and humility possess God, who is an inexhaustible ocean of beatitude.

GRACIOUSLY HEAR, O GOD, the fervent prayers we offer Thee for the suffering souls in purgatory, who, not having satisfied Thy justice, confide in Thine infinite mercy and our intercessions. Extend unto them Thy consolations, and redeem them, through Christ our Lord. Amen.

Eternal rest grant unto them, O Lord, and let perpetual light shine upon them. May they rest in peace. Amen.

"Ingratitude has never entered heaven."

— *WORDS OF THE HOLY SOULS TO*
ST. MARGARET MARY ALACOQUE

Day Twenty-Eight
Perseverance in Prayer

"BE CONSTANT in prayer."

— *ROMANS 12:12*

IF WE WERE "in constant pursuit of love," we would obtain the vision of God for many a soul in purgatory. Karl Rahner, in *Encounters With Silence*, shares this soliloquy:

> Their silence is their loudest call, because it is the echo of God's silence.... They are silent because they live, just as we chatter so loudly to try to make ourselves forget that we are dying. Their silence is really their call, the assurance of their immortal love for us. O silent God ... God of those who are silently summoning us to enter into Your life, never let us forget our dead or our living. May our love and faithfulness to them be a pledge of our belief in You, the God of eternal life.

> Let us not be deaf to the call of their silence, which is the surest and sincerest word of their love. May this word of theirs continue to accompany us, even

after they have taken leave of us to enter into You, for thus their love comes all the closer to us.

When we pray, "Grant them eternal rest, O Lord, and let Thy perpetual light shine upon them," let our words be only the echo of the prayer of love that they themselves are speaking in the silence of eternity.

GRACIOUSLY HEAR, O GOD, the fervent prayers we offer Thee for the suffering souls in purgatory, who, not having satisfied Thy justice, confide in Thine infinite mercy and our intercessions. Extend unto them Thy consolations, and redeem them, through Christ our Lord. Amen.

Eternal rest grant unto them, O Lord, and let perpetual light shine upon them. May they rest in peace. Amen.

"*The fruit of silence is prayer.*
The fruit of prayer is faith.
The fruit of faith is love.
The fruit of love is service.
The fruit of service is peace."

— *BLESSED MOTHER TERESA OF CALCUTTA*

Day Twenty-Nine
The Honor and Glory of God

"HE HAS SHOWED YOU, O man, what is good; and what does the LORD require of you but to do justice, and to love kindness, and to walk humbly with your God?"

— *MICAH 6:8*

BLESSED MARY OF PROVIDENCE asked, "How could I help God? He is our helper. How can we help Him? He gives me everything. How could I give Him everything?" And the answer that grace put into the saint's heart was always, "By paying the debts of the souls in purgatory."

Begin today to pay the debts of the poor souls — through prayer, fasting, and good works.

GRACIOUSLY HEAR, O GOD, the fervent prayers we offer Thee for the suffering souls in purgatory, who, not having satisfied Thy justice, confide in Thine infinite mercy and our intercessions. Extend unto them Thy consolations, and redeem them, through Christ our Lord. Amen.

Eternal rest grant unto them, O Lord, and let perpetual light shine upon them. May they rest in peace. Amen.

"Of all prayers, the most meritorious, the most acceptable to God, are prayers for the dead, because they imply all the works of charity, both corporal and spiritual."

— ST. THOMAS AQUINAS

Day Thirty
Heroic Act of Charity

"Therefore be imitators of God, as beloved children. And walk in love, as Christ loved us and gave himself up for us, a fragrant offering and sacrifice to God."

— *EPHESIANS 5:1-2*

THE HEROIC ACT of charity is an offering of all works of satisfaction we may gain during life and all the suffrages that may be offered for us after death. We place this offering in the hands of Our Blessed Lady, leaving her to apply it as she sees fit for the release of the souls in purgatory. This does not prevent us from working or praying for ourselves, our relatives, or others. This act does not oblige under pain of sin, and it can be revoked at any time. It may be without any special formula.

A key advantage of this heroic act is that it increases our eternal glory, the possession in a greater degree of God for all eternity. The heroic act is an exchange of glory for merit, of purgatory for heaven, of time for eternity, of pain for glory and for God. It is one of the greatest sacrifices we can make to God. We take upon ourselves to pay "the last penny," the whole of the debt that we now owe, and may ever owe, to God.

Offering of the Heroic Act

O HOLY AND ADORABLE TRINITY, desiring to cooperate in the deliverance of the souls in purgatory, and to testify, to my devotion to the Blessed Virgin Mary, I cede and renounce in behalf of the holy souls, all the satisfactory value of all my works during life, and all the suffrages which may be given to me after my death, consigning them entirely into the hands of the Blessed Virgin, that she may apply them according to her good pleasure to the souls of the faithful departed, whom she desires to deliver from their sufferings. Deign, O my God, to accept and bless this offering which I make to Thee at this moment. Amen.

GRACIOUSLY HEAR, O GOD, the fervent prayers we offer Thee for the suffering souls in purgatory, who, not having satisfied Thy justice, confide in Thine infinite mercy and our intercessions. Extend unto them Thy consolations, and redeem them, through Christ our Lord. Amen.

Eternal rest grant unto them, O Lord, and let perpetual light shine upon them. May they rest in peace. Amen.

"There is an intense participation in life between us and the sisters and brothers who are in heavenly glory, or who are still being purified after death."

— *POPE JOHN PAUL II*

$\mathcal{M}$emorial Prayer for the Suffering Souls in Purgatory

ALMIGHTY GOD, Father of goodness and love, have mercy on the poor suffering souls and grant Thy aid:

To my dear parents and ancestors,
  Jesus, Mary, Joseph! My Jesus, mercy.
To my brothers and sisters and other
  near relatives,
  Jesus, etc.
To my benefactors, spiritual and temporal,
To my former friends and colleagues,
To all for whom love or duty bids me pray,
To those who have suffered disadvantage or
  harm through me,
To those who have offended me,
To all those who are especially beloved by You,
To those whose release is at hand,
To those who desire most to be united with You,
To those who endure the greatest suffering,
To those whose release is most remote,
To those who are least remembered,

To those who are most deserving on account of
their services to the Church,

To the rich, who now are the most destitute,

To the mighty, who now are as lowly as servants,

To the blind, who now see their folly,

To the frivolous, who spent their time in idleness,

To the poor, who did not seek the treasures
of heaven,

To the tepid, who devoted little time to prayer,

To the indolent, who were negligent in
performing good works,

To those of little faith, who neglected the
frequent reception of the sacraments,

To the habitual sinners, who owe their salvation
to a miracle of grace,

To parents who failed to watch over their
children,

To superiors who were not solicitous for the
salvation of those entrusted to them,

To the souls of those who strove for hardly
anything but riches and pleasures,

To the worldly minded, who failed to use their
wealth and talents in the service of God,

To those who witnessed the death of others,
but would not think of their own,

To those who did not provide for the great
    journey beyond, and the days of tribulation,
To those whose judgment is so severe because
    of the great things entrusted to them,
To the popes, rulers, kings, and princes,
To the bishops and their counselors,
To my teachers and spiritual advisers,
To the deceased priests of this diocese,
To all the priests and Religious of the whole
    Catholic Church,
To the defenders of the holy faith,
To those who died on the battlefield,
To those who are buried in the sea,
To those who died of stroke or heart attack,
To those who died without the last rites
    of the Church,
To those who shall die within the next
    twenty-four hours,
To my own poor soul when I shall have to
    appear before Thy judgment seat.

O LORD, grant eternal rest to all the souls of
the faithful departed, and let perpetual light shine
upon them. May they rest in peace. Amen.

King of Glory

THE KING OF GLORY will show them favor.
The Virgin Mary will befriend them, the Twelve
Apostles will bid them welcome. O riches, more
than they can ever spend. The angels will play
Paradise music. God's poor, rejoicing, will in full
voice sing. Far better this than a world unthink-
ing. What joy to souls, the smile of heaven's
King.

Gone Only From My Sight

I AM STANDING on the seashore.
Suddenly a ship at my side
spreads her white sails to the morning breeze,
and starts out for the blue ocean.
She is an object of beauty and strength,
and I stand and watch her
until at length she is only a ribbon of white
   cloud

just above where sea and sky mingle with
    each other.
Then someone at my side says,
"There! She's gone!"

Gone where?
Gone from my sight — that is all.
She is just as large in mast and hull and spar
as she was when she left my side,
and just as able to bear her load of living freight
to the place of destination.
Her diminished size is in me, not in her,
and just at the moment when someone at my
    side says,
"There! She's gone!"
there are other voices ready to take the glad
    shout,
"There! She comes!"

And that is dying.

*Words found in the wallet of Colonel Marcus, of the
Israeli Army, when he was killed in action on June
11, 1948.*

Other Spiritual Treasures to Aid the Suffering Souls

• HOLY WATER is a sacramental that remits venial sin. It benefits the soul and body for the living and brings consolation to the souls of the departed. The holy souls long for holy water. If we desire to make a host of intercessors for ourselves, let us always remember the holy souls at the holy water font. The holy souls nearest to heaven may need the sprinkling of only one drop to release them.

Use Holy Water as follows: Dip your fingers into the holy water and say, "By this holy water and by Thy precious blood, wash away all my sin, O Lord, and relieve the souls in purgatory," and then make the Sign of the Cross.

• JOIN THE PIOUS UNION OF ST. JOSEPH, patron of the suffering and dying. This association is dedicated to praying a universal prayer for the dying. To become a member, contact:

Pious Union of St. Joseph
971 E. Michigan Ave.
Grass Lake, MI 49240-9210
phone: (517) 522-8017
e-mail: piousunion@aol.com

St. Joseph repays us generously if we come to the rescue of the suffering souls. Holy Communions offered to him for seven consecutive Sundays in honor of the holy souls is a powerful devotion.

• GREGORIAN MASSES are thirty Masses offered consecutively for one deceased soul. Contact the local Missions Office in your diocese for details. You are encouraged to put these Masses in your will.

About the Author

WITH THIS TITLE, Susan Tassone adds a fourth Our Sunday Visitor book to her list of literary accomplishments. Her first work, *The Way of the Cross for the Holy Souls in Purgatory*, has sold more than 50,000 copies. This was followed by her *Praying in the Presence of Our Lord for the Holy Souls*, which was on the Catholic best-sellers list twice; it is one of a number of

POPE JOHN PAUL II BESTOWS HIS APOSTOLIC BLESSING ON SUSAN TASSONE'S WORK AND HER BOOK *PRAYING IN THE PRESENCE OF OUR LORD FOR THE HOLY SOULS*.

books in the *Praying in the Presence of Our Lord* series by various authors.

Susan, who holds a master's degree in religious education from Loyola University Chicago and is a consultant for a major nonprofit philanthropic organization in that city, has had the honor and privilege of being granted two private audiences with His Holiness Pope John Paul II.

Contact Our Sunday Visitor (toll-free: 1-800-348-2440; e-mail: osvbooks@osv.com; website: www.osv.com) and ask for these works by Susan Tassone:

- *The Way of the Cross for the Holy Souls in Purgatory*, 0-87973-411-6 (411), paper, 48 pages.
- *Praying in the Presence of Our Lord for the Holy Souls*, 0-87973-921-5 (921), paper, 176 pages.
- *The Rosary for the Holy Souls in Purgatory*, 1-931709-42-4 (T25), paper, 192 pages.
- *Prayers of Intercession for the Holy Souls*, 1-59276-054-6 (M105), audio; 1-59276-055-4 (M106), CD.

Our Sunday Visitor ...
Your Source for Discovering
the Riches of the Catholic Faith

Our Sunday Visitor has an extensive line of materials for young children, teens, and adults. Our books, Bibles, booklets, CD-ROMs, audios, and videos are available in bookstores worldwide.

To receive a FREE full-line catalog or for more information, call **Our Sunday Visitor** at **1-800-348-2440, ext. 3**. Or write, **Our Sunday Visitor** / 200 Noll Plaza / Huntington, IN 46750.

Please send me ___ A catalog
Please send me materials on:
___ Apologetics and catechetics
___ Prayer books
___ The family
___ Reference works
___ Heritage and the saints
___ The parish
Name _____
Address _____ Apt. _____
City _____ State _____ Zip _____
Telephone ( ) _____

A43BBBBP

Please send a friend ___ A catalog
Please send me materials on:
___ Apologetics and catechetics
___ Prayer books
___ The family
___ Reference works
___ Heritage and the saints
___ The parish
Name _____
Address _____ Apt. _____
City _____ State _____ Zip _____
Telephone ( ) _____

A43BBBBP

OurSundayVisitor

200 Noll Plaza, Huntington, IN 46750
Toll free: **1-800-348-2440**
Website: www.osv.com